Seaside

Katie Dicker

LABURNUM PRESS

Laburnum House Educational Ltd
Caldicott Drive
Heapham Road Industrial Estate
Gainsborough
DN21 1FJ

British Library Cataloguing in Publication Data (CIP) exists for this title.

ISBN 9781909850064
Printed by EDELVIVES, Spain
Printed on chlorine-free paper from sustainably managed sources

Developed and Created for Laburnum Press by White-Thomson Publishing Ltd, 2 St Andrews Place Lewes, East Sussex, BN7 1UP

For Joshua

Acknowledgements
Educational consultant: Sue Palmer Med FRSA FEA
Project Manager: Katie Dicker
Picture research: Amy Sparks
Design: Balley Design Ltd
Creative director: Simon Balley
Designer/Illustrator: Michelle Tilly/Andrew Li

Contents

Day trip

4

Pages 4–5: Day trip
Explain to children that the seaside is a place where the land meets the sea. Show them different stretches of coastline on a map. You could take children to a local beach to experience the seaside for themselves. Alternatively, you could make your own beach. Fill a tray (three-quarters) with sand or pebbles and add a plastic divider. Add 'sea' water and move the tray back and forth to make waves.

Pages 6–7: Sand and pebbles
Children may enjoy looking for stones with special shapes or markings – at the beach or from a collection of pebbles. Help the children to make a paperweight by varnishing their stones. Children may also enjoy activities at the beach, such as throwing small pebbles into the water, knocking a tin can off a pile of stones or making a sand boat.

Pages 8–9: Seaweed and shells
Encourage children to collect seashells and group them in colour or order of size. Use books or the Internet to help the children identify where the shells come from. You could also collect some dried seaweed. Draw a face on a piece of card and use shells for the features and seaweed as 'hair'.

Pages 10–11: In the water
Children may enjoy making their own sunglasses, sun hat or arm bands from card and tissue paper. Talk to children about the importance of water and sun safety at the seaside. What other safety precautions are important? What behaviour makes the seaside a safe place for others to use?

Pages 12–13: Wind and waves
Children may enjoy playing a game about waves. Ask the children to hold the edges of a blue sheet and to make 'waves' by slowly moving the sheet up and down. Children take it in turns to run underneath the sheet without being caught by the waves. Children may also enjoy making their own coloured kite or windmill to use on a windy day.

Pages 14–15: Rockpools
Help children to make their own rockpool in a tray of water, and their own rockpool creatures using self-hardening clay and waterproof paint. Children could play a game by hiding the creatures in their rockpool and asking a friend to find the different animals.

Pages 16–17: Sealife
Collect a series of photographs of seaside creatures, cut from magazines or printed from the Internet. Make a collage of your creatures on the wall, creating an 'underwater' effect with blue and green tissue paper. Use books or the Internet to help the children identify the different creatures.

Pages 18–19: Fishing
Encourage children to draw a seaside picture with sand, sea and sky. Help them to cut a slit for the horizon. Children could make their own boats from card with a thin strip from the hull as a handle. Put the boats 'through' the horizon to show them 'bobbing' along the water. Children may also enjoy making their own fishing rods or nets from strong card and string.

Pages 20–21: Fun and games
Children may enjoy acting out a day at the seaside. Encourage children to make the sounds of the sea or the seagulls, to walk barefoot and to act out feeling hot in the sun. Children may also enjoy drawing a postcard about a day at the beach, talking about the games they played, the sights they saw and the sounds they heard.

Index

Picture acknowledgements:
Alamy: 10 (ACE Stock Limited), 18 (PCL); **Corbis:** 9 (Paul Barton/zefa), 11 (Paul Barton/zefa), 17 (Randy Faris), 21 (Rolf Bruderer); **Getty Images:** cover girls (Stockbyte), 6 (Jose Luis Pelaez Inc), 13 (Stockbyte), 14 (Joson Photo LLC), 19 (Christopher Robbins), 20 (Gallo Images/Guy Bubb); **IStockphoto:** cover beach (Alberto Pomares), cover sky (JLF Capture), 15 starfish, 15 anemone, 15 limpet; **Photolibrary:** 8 (Santa Clara); **Shutterstock:** 2–3 beach (Christian Wheatley), 4 (Monkey Business Images), 5 (Mikhail Tchkheidze), 7 (Jozsef Szasz-Fabian), 12 (sculpies), 15 crab (Lijuan Guo), 16 (Manuel Fernandes), 22–23 beach (Christian Wheatley), 24 beach (Christian Wheatley).

Sand and pebbles

This sand is good for building.

bucket →

6

How TALL can you make

a pile of pebbles?

balancing

7

Seaweed and shells

What different types
of shells can you find?

itchy!

What does **seaweed** feel like?

In the water

piggy back

The sea water is cool on a hot day.

10

Wind and waves

Faster!

A windy day is good for surfing on the waves.

How high can you fly a kite?

13

Rockpools

What is it?

At low tide, this beach is full of rockpools.

How do these rockpool creatures move?

15

Now make a shape
like a starfish!

17

Fishing

These boats are used to catch fish at sea.

Sparklers books are designed to support and extend the learning of young children. The **Food We Eat** titles won a Practical Pre-School Silver Award and the **Body Moves** titles won a Practical Pre-School Gold Award. The books' high-interest subjects link in to the Early Years curriculum and beyond. Find out more about Early Years and reading with children from the National Literacy Trust (www.literacytrust.org.uk).

Themed titles

Seaside is one of four **Out and About** titles that encourage children to explore outdoor spaces. The other titles are:

Park   **Garden**   **Wood**

Areas of learning

Each **Out and About** title helps to support the following Foundation Stage areas of learning:
Personal, Social and Emotional Development
Communication, Language and Literacy
Mathematical Development
Knowledge and Understanding of the World
Physical Development
Creative Development

Making the most of reading time

When reading with younger children, take time to explore the pictures together. Ask children to find, identify, count or describe different objects. Point out colours and textures. Allow quiet spaces in your reading so that children can ask questions or repeat your words. Try pausing mid-sentence so that children can predict the next word. This sort of participation develops early reading skills.

Follow the words with your finger as you read. The main text is in Infant Sassoon, a clear, friendly font designed for children learning to read and write. The labels and sound effects add fun and give the opportunity to distinguish between levels of communication. Where appropriate, labels, sound effects or main text may be presented phonically. Encourage children to imitate the sounds.

As you read the book, you can also take the opportunity to talk about the book itself with appropriate vocabulary such as "page", "cover", "back", "front", "photograph", "label" and "page number".

You can also extend children's learning by using the books as a springboard for discussion and further activities. There are a few suggestions on the facing page.